CHRISTOPHER JORDAN

BASEBALL ANIMALS

FENN
TUNDRA

MAJOR LEAGUE BASEBALL

For my little baseball fans, Stewart, Duncan and Jacqueline — Love, Daddy

Published in Canada by Fenn/Tundra of Tundra Books, a division of Random House of Canada Limited,
One Toronto Street, Suite 300, Toronto, Ontario M5C 2V6

Published in the United States by Fenn/Tundra of Tundra Books of Northern New York,
P.O. Box 1030, Plattsburgh, New York 12901

Library of Congress Control Number: 2012913477

Library and Archives Canada Cataloguing in Publication

Jordan, Christopher, 1972-
        Baseball animals / Christopher Jordan.

ISBN 978-1-77049-474-9

        1. Animals – Juvenile literature. 2. Birds – Juvenile literature.
3. Major League Baseball (Organization) – Juvenile literature.
4. Baseball – Juvenile literature. I. Title.

QL49.J646 2014   j590   C2012-905280-9

Image Credits (photographer)
Getty Images Sport: Pages 4 (Otto Greule Jr), 6 (Brad White), 8 (Dilip Vishwanat), 10 (J. Meric), 12 (Norm Hall), 14 (Ronald
C. Modra), 16 (Leon Halip), 17 (Mike Dunning/Dorling Kindersley) 18 (David Banks), 20 (Thearon W. Henderson), 22 (Left:
Rob Carr / Right: Pouya Dianat); *Shutterstock:* Pages 5 (Mike Truchon), 7 (Elliotte Rusty Harold), 9 (StudioSmart), 15 (Eric
Isselee), 19 (Beneda Miroslav), 21 (Paul Barnwell); *Corbis:* Pages 3 (Visuals Unlimited), 11 (Ocean), 13 (Visuals Unlimited)

Edited by Dorothy Milne

www.tundrabooks.com

Printed and bound in Hong Kong

1 2 3 4 5 6   19 18 17 16 15 14

?

Which MLB team was named after a black bird with a bright orange underbelly?

This bird likes to perch high in the treetops and prefers to eat dark-colored fruit such as cherries or purple grapes.

The **Baltimore Orioles** were named after the official state bird of Maryland. Their team logo has changed many times over the years. Sometimes it has looked like a real oriole, and sometimes it has been a cartoon version.

?

Which MLB team shares its name with a songbird that loves acorns?

 This blue, black and white bird is thought to be responsible for spreading the oak tree across North America.

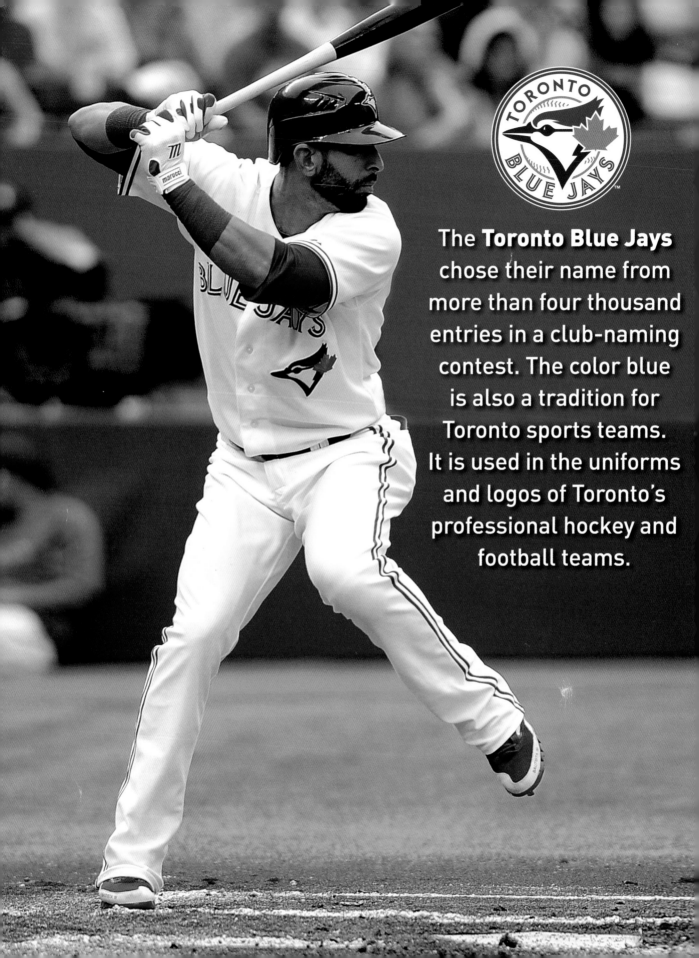

The **Toronto Blue Jays** chose their name from more than four thousand entries in a club-naming contest. The color blue is also a tradition for Toronto sports teams. It is used in the uniforms and logos of Toronto's professional hockey and football teams.

?

Which MLB team shares its name with a common red bird found in North and South America?

You can easily tell the difference between the male and female bird. The male's feathers are a much brighter red!

Although the **St. Louis Cardinals** were not named after the bird, their original red uniforms were described as being a brilliant cardinal red — and the name stuck!

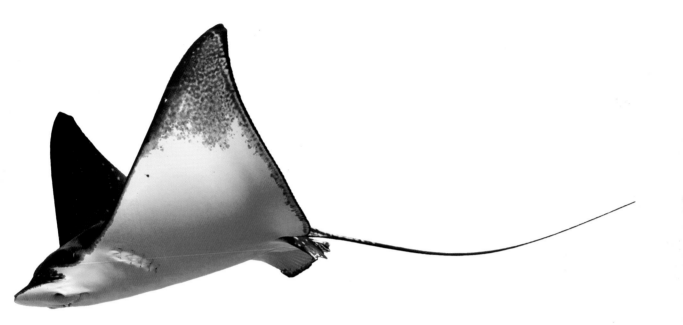

?

**Which MLB team was
originally named after
a member of the
manta ray family?**

The largest manta ray ever found was
25 feet (7.62 m) wide and weighed
more than 5,952 pounds (2,700 kg)!

The **Tampa Bay Rays** were originally named after the devil ray. This type of manta ray lives, on average, for twenty years. The team still wears a devil ray patch on their uniform.

Which MLB team is named after a strong and venomous snake?

This snake can grow up to 4 feet (1.21 m) in length and has black and white bands on its tail, just like a raccoon.

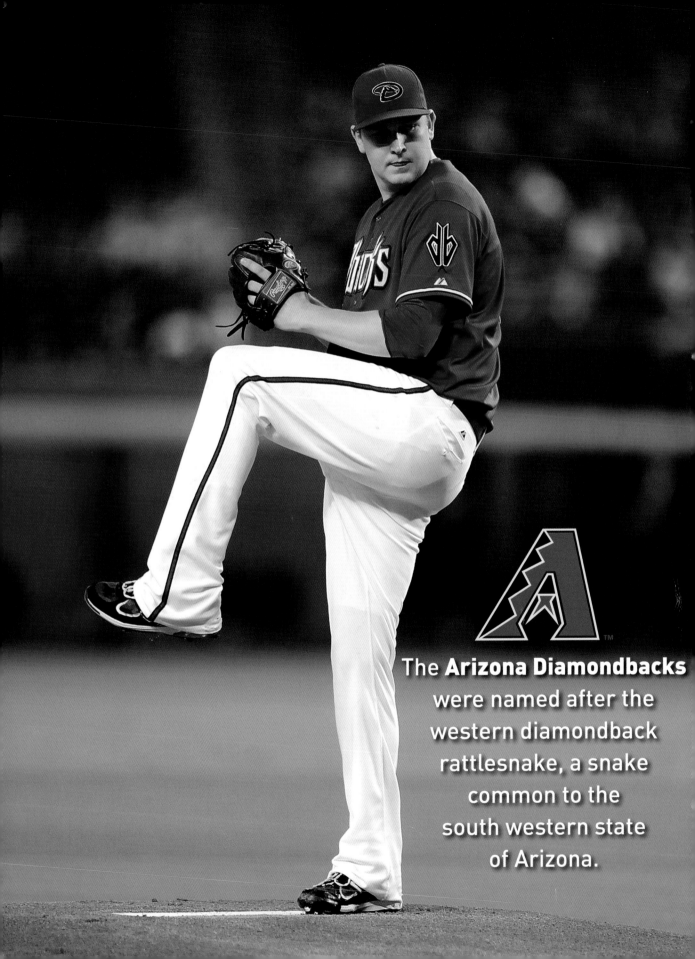

The **Arizona Diamondbacks** were named after the western diamondback rattlesnake, a snake common to the south western state of Arizona.

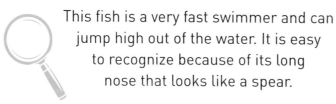

This fish is a very fast swimmer and can jump high out of the water. It is easy to recognize because of its long nose that looks like a spear.

Which MLB team was named after a sport fish that can grow to a length of 20 feet (6.09 m) and weigh in at a whopping 1,807 pounds (820 kg)?

MIAMI

The **Miami Marlins** were named after the marlin, one of the most common types of fish in southern Florida.

This animal is the largest member of the cat family and is an excellent hunter.

?

Which MLB team shares its name with an animal known for its orange fur with black stripes?

The **Detroit Tigers** were not
named after the animal but one of
the oldest military units in Michigan,
known as the Tigers.

Which MLB team shares its name with a newborn bear?

Black bear babies weigh just 10 ounces (less than a pound) at birth, but they can grow to be 500 pounds (227 kg) as adults!

The **Chicago Cubs** were named to reflect the youth and playfulness of their players, as well as the incredible strength of the black bear.

?

Which MLB team shows a popular performing circus animal on its alternate logo?

This animal is the largest land mammal in the world. It is easily recognized because of its very big ears and long trunk.

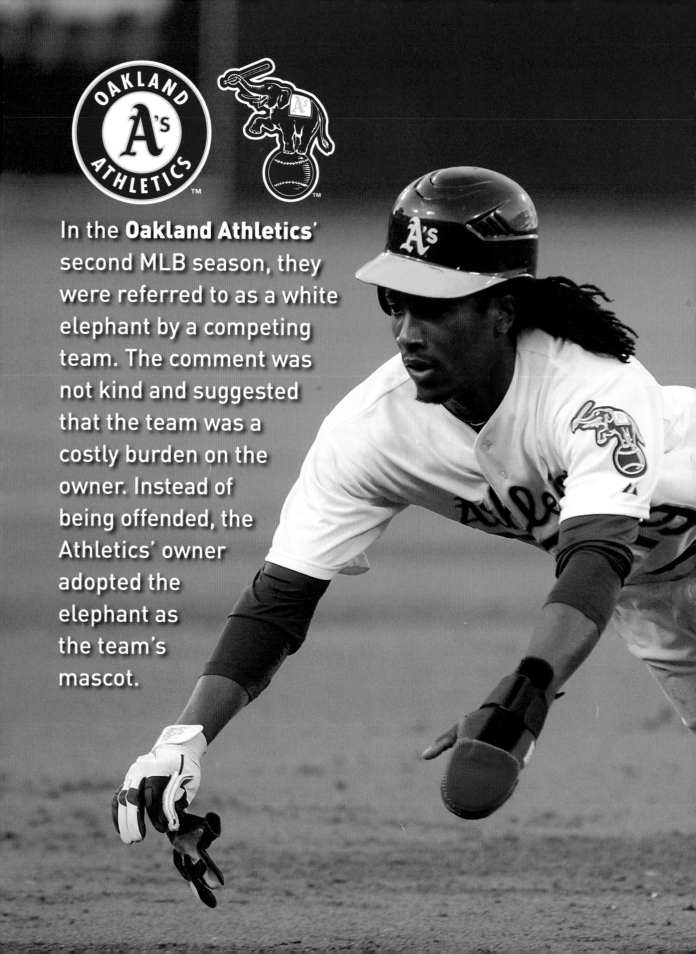

In the **Oakland Athletics'** second MLB season, they were referred to as a white elephant by a competing team. The comment was not kind and suggested that the team was a costly burden on the owner. Instead of being offended, the Athletics' owner adopted the elephant as the team's mascot.

In spite of its name, this bird is not bald. Its head is covered in soft white feathers, and it has an average wingspan of 8 feet (2.43 m). This bird's amazing eyesight allows it to see prey from very far away.

?

On which Major League Baseball logos can you find this majestic bird?

The bald eagle appears on both the American League and the National League logos. It became the emblem of the United States of America on June 20, 1782.

APPENDIX OF MLB TEAMS AND LOGOS

AMERICAN LEAGUE

 Baltimore Orioles: Baltimore, Maryland. Founded 1894

 Boston Red Sox: Boston, Massachusetts. Founded 1901

 Chicago White Sox: Chicago, Illinois. Founded 1894

 Cleveland Indians: Cleveland, Ohio. Founded 1894

 Detroit Tigers: Detroit, Michigan. Founded 1894

 Houston Astros: Houston, Texas. Founded 1962 (NL)

 Kansas City Royals: Kansas City, Missouri. Founded 1969

 Los Angeles Angels of Anaheim: Anaheim, California. Founded 1961

 Minnesota Twins: Minneapolis, Minnesota. Founded 1894

 New York Yankees: Bronx, New York. Founded 1901

 Oakland Athletics: Oakland, California. Founded 1901

 Seattle Mariners: Seattle, Washington. Founded 1977

 Tampa Bay Rays: St. Petersburg, Florida. Founded 1998

 Texas Rangers: Arlington, Texas. Founded 1961

 Toronto Blue Jays: Toronto, Ontario, Canada. Founded 1977

NATIONAL LEAGUE

 Arizona Diamondbacks: Phoenix, Arizona. Founded 1998

 Atlanta Braves: Atlanta, Georgia. Founded 1871

 Chicago Cubs: Chicago, Illinois. Founded 1870

 Cincinnati Reds: Cincinnati, Ohio. Founded 1882

 Colorado Rockies: Denver, Colorado. Founded 1993

 Los Angeles Dodgers: Los Angeles, California. Founded 1883

 Miami Marlins: Miami, Florida. Founded 1993

 Milwaukee Brewers: Milwaukee, Wisconsin. Founded 1969 (AL)

 New York Mets: Flushing, New York. Founded 1962

 Philadelphia Phillies: Philadelphia, Pennsylvania. Founded 1883

 Pittsburgh Pirates: Pittsburgh, Pennsylvania. Founded 1882

 San Diego Padres: San Diego, California. Founded 1969

 San Francisco Giants: San Francisco, California. Founded 1883

 St. Louis Cardinals: St. Louis, Missouri. Founded 1882

 Washington Nationals: Washington, D.C. Founded 1969